PREPARATION FOR GLORY

Afflictions, trials, tribulations, and discipline

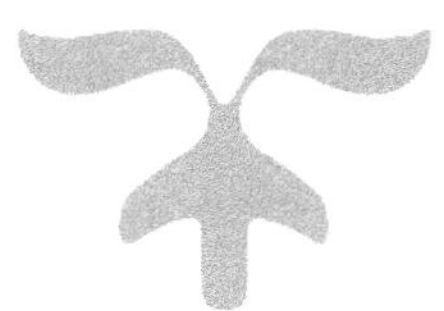

Luis M. Orta AM., M. Div.

Library of Congress Cataloging-in-Publication Data
Name: Luis M. Orta A.M., M.Div.
Title: Preparation for Glory: Afflictions. trials, tribulations, and discipline.
Identifiers
PCN- 2025909297
LCCN- 2025909297
ISBN- 979-8-218-66419-0

Dedicated to all who

suffer and feel that there is no hope.

Acknowledgements

I would like to acknowledge the matriarch of my immediate family, Norma Iris Orta Echevarria, who taught me to pray at the age of three, which is where my Christian roots began. She is a phenomenal woman, who worked two jobs for thirty-five years to support my brother and me after enduring sixteen years of violence and instability. A strong, resilient woman, who is seventy-five years old and still involved in my life. I love her dearly.

I would also like to acknowledge my paternal grandmother, Rev. Inez Suarez, for being the solid rock of faith that she has been since my childhood. She was a missionary bringing the Gospel to the unchurched and building churches wherever she settled. She organized the church in the jungle surrounding Medellin, Columbia, where the native people of the territory were crushing cocoa leaves with gasoline to make the paste to sell to the cartel to refine into cocaine.

After I finished the book and sent it in for editing, I lost complete control of my right hand, making me a full quadriplegic. When the editors would send my work back to approve the editing, my caregiver, LeAnne Pafford, was a great help in approving and correcting the edits, while caring for me.

In 1978 at the age of 12, I accepted Christ as my Lord and savior and was baptized in full immersion at the First Baptist Church of Hammond, IN, becoming a son of God.

About the Book

"Preparation for Glory: Afflictions, Trials, Tribulations, and Discipline" by Luis M. Orta explores the idea that afflictions and hardships are not always a result of sin but can be used to purify and strengthen one's faith for the Glory of God. The book delves into individual experiences and theological insights to understand the relationship between suffering and spiritual growth.

After his diagnosis with multiple sclerosis in 1996, the onset of the disease was in 1994. Luis struggled to understand why Christians seemed to suffer more than others. After his diagnosis, Luis stopped running around the streets, selling and using drugs. He returned to his Christian roots and studied psychology, psychotherapy, and theology to understand why the good and the bad suffer in this world. Luis has had quadriplegia since 2006, when he was 41 years old. He now has lupus and has been sick for over 30 years.

Preparation for Glory is a self-help book in the religion category that attempts to explain why God afflicts humanity and allows us to suffer worldly problems. The author mentions that God deliberately allows this to prepare us for His blessings.

The author put years of experience and labor into this work and is passionate about teaching others about the Bible and God's intentions. Luis is quadriplegic and can only type with one finger. The author is well abreast of Scripture.

ιχθύς

Table of Contents

Preface

I was taught that good things happen to people who do good things and terrible things happen to people who do awful things.

Reading the Bible and reflecting on my life has helped me understand that afflictions, trials, tribulations, and discipline can occur in anyone's life at any time. I struggled to understand why God allows believers to suffer, along with nonbelievers, and I found the answers woven throughout the Bible.

My purpose for writing this book is to help the reader understand that any unpleasant experiences in our lives can help us become more reliable people here on earth and prepare us for eternal Glory with God.

How can we stand in the presence of God if we are weak and unclean? Afflictions, trials, tribulations, and discipline can bring us closer to godliness if we stop focusing on what we may have done to bring about the suffering and begin to focus on how we can get closer to God while enduring our pain.

This book contains Bible verses that will help the reader understand that many personalities in the Bible suffered so that their faith will be stronger or correct their mistakes to take hold of all that God has prepared for them. First, God prepares a blessing; then, God prepares us to receive the benefit.

Enduring suffering can help prepare us to receive God's blessings. This book is a short book directing us toward different situations within the Bible where God allows afflictions, trials, tribulations, and suffering to be part of our lives to draw us closer.

Introduction

Woe is Me

A Vision of God in the Temple

> ***6*** *[1] In the year that King Uzziah died, I saw the Lord sitting on a throne, high and lofty, and the hem of his robe filled the temple.[2] Seraphs were in attendance above him; each had six wings: with two, they covered their faces, and with two, they covered their feet, and with two, they flew. [3] And one called to another and said: "Holy, holy, holy is the LORD of hosts; the whole earth is full of his glory." .[4] The pivots on the thresholds shook at the voices of those who called, and the house filled with smoke. [5] And I said: "Woe is me! I am lost, for I am a man of unclean lips, and I live among a people of unclean lips; yet my eyes have seen the King, the LORD of hosts!"*
> **(Isaiah 6:1-5)**

When we read the Bible, we learn that prophets have had visions of God before they spoke to God's people. I have always been fascinated by these visions because of the way God is described. I have read in the Bible that human beings could never see God and live, so I am eager to learn about the experience when I read about those visions. I want to know all there is to understand when it comes to biblical personalities and their beliefs in God because I am interested in how they respond to being in the presence of God.

Of all the recorded visions of God, Isaiah's response is one of the most appropriate. Isaiah is overwhelmed, and all his imperfections rise to the surface, and he responds in the only way that he can, "Woe is me." Isaiah's response challenged me to reflect on how unworthy we are to be in the presence of God. In **Psalm 8:4,** God is asked: ***"What are human beings that you are mindful of them, or mortals, that you care for them?"*** I ask myself a similar question.

Why does God even bother to give us visions and prepare us to be blessed? We are creatures serving our selfish needs and, in most cases, come to God to avoid physical suffering or to avoid eternal damnation. The answer that God impressed upon my heart was that God loves us, and all that God allows is out of love.

God created us body, soul, and spirit to experience both the physical and the spirit world, and sometimes, we need to get a glimpse of the spirit world to effect change in the physical world. Isaiah's vision of the spirit world overwhelmed him because it became clear to him that he was not prepared to be in the spirit world with God, and those whom he was commissioned to give revelation about God were even less prepared. Isaiah's response was two-fold. Isaiah was concerned with his unworthiness of God's love, and now he had to explain to his people that they were unworthy and needed to be prepared before they could receive the Glory that God had for them.

What a monumental task. Who was Isaiah that God would commission him to complete such a mission? Isaiah's self-awareness allowed him to realize that he was unworthy and unclean. However, God knew the contents of Isaiah's heart. Isaiah showed self-awareness, and that is crucial for anyone who needs to change their self-image and behavior. Being aware that we are unworthy of God's grace and love can lead us to Christ and prepare us for God's Glory.

The premise of this work is that God allows suffering to come upon us, His children, to prepare us for the blessings ahead. While God allows adversity in our lives, the enemy of God and all that God created is also at work as the enemy of our souls to distract us from God's purpose and entice us to curse God and sin against God so that we can be separated from God. This adversary of God is Lucifer (i.e., Satan). Satan is a sworn and eternal enemy of our souls and has been separated from God for eternity. He is willing to do anything he can to separate us from God.

However, God has put strict limitations on Satan. In this book, I write, "No matter how evil the plans, Satan can never afflict us unless: (a) we purposefully look to do evil, and if we do, we are in Satan's will, or (b) God allows Satan to afflict us. God has Satan restricted from doing us harm without permission." This is my opinion according to my experiences, education, and my faith tradition.

Why does Satan (i.e., Lucifer) hate us so much? Because we have a chance to be in God's Kingdom, and Satan lost that forever. Lucifer (i.e., Morning Star, found in ***Isaiah 14:12-21***) was a glorious angel who led other angels in worshipping God. Lucifer illuminated God's Throne with praise and worship, but free will and desires blinded Lucifer, who was full of pride and wanted to occupy God's Throne (***1 Timothy 3:6***). Lucifer wanted to be greater than God. Lucifer's free will and personal desires resulted in the war in Heaven that ended with Lucifer and one-third of the angels losing their status as angels and being expelled from heaven (***Ezekiel 28:12-19, Luke 10:18, Revelation12:7-10***). War is destructive, so it would be fair to say that the angels staying in Heaven do not want to deal with another rebellion. The way we endure suffering can purge our harmful personal desires from our consciousness and free will and prepare us for God's Glory.

1

The Bitter Made Sweet

In the Book of Exodus, we meet Moses, one of the Bible's most revered personalities. Moses was born a Hebrew enslaved person. He was placed in a basket and put in the Nile River by his mother to save his life after Pharaoh instituted a plan to kill all firstborn male children born to the Hebrews to reduce the Hebrew population, which had grown dramatically in the over 400 years that the Hebrews were in Egypt. Pharaoh's daughter found Moses and raised him as a Prince of Egypt ***(Exodus 2:1-10)***. This book tells the tale of how God delivered His chosen people from bondage in Egypt. The Hebrews are descendants of Abraham, Isaac, and Jacob and were slaves to Pharaoh, who did not care how Jacob's son Joseph had helped Egypt 400 years earlier. In this book, the Hebrew's bitter bondage turned into sweet freedom.

While he was a Prince of Egypt, Moses rescued an older Hebrew from death by killing an Egyptian Slave-Master and had to flee Egypt. 40 years later, God commissioned Moses to deliver the Hebrews out of Egypt.

Through Moses, God gives us the Hebrew Laws and instructions on living godly lives and relating to each other. These statutes defined a just and proper way of life for the Hebrews and us today. Laws of God also look after the well-being of the poor and the oppressed, and they address criminal justice issues, ecological concerns, and equality for all. In Exodus, we also learn how to gain access to God for repentance of our sins.

While wandering in the wilderness, the Hebrew's water supply runs out, and the people quickly forget all that God had done for them and begin to complain. By the 15th chapter of Exodus, God had done remarkable things to deliver the Hebrews from Egypt, but they still complained, so God tested them at Marah. It is easy to forget that God is with us when difficulties arise.

Bitter Water Made Sweet

15 *22 Then Moses ordered Israel to set out from the Red*
Sea, and they went into Shur's wilderness. They went for
three days through the desert and found no water. 23 When
they came to Marah; they could not drink the water of
Marah because it was bitter. That is why it was called
Marah. 24 And, the people complained against Moses,
saying, "What shall we drink?" 25 He cried out to the
LORD, and the LORD showed him a piece of wood; he
threw it into the water, and the water became sweet. There,
the LORD made a statute and an ordinance for them, and
there he put them to the test. 26He said, "If you will listen

carefully to the voice of the LORD your God, and do what is right in his sight, and give heed to his commandments and keep all His statutes, I will not bring upon you any of the diseases that I brought upon the Egyptians; for I am the LORD who heals you."[27] Then they came to Elim, where there were twelve springs of water and seventy palm trees, and they camped there by the stream.
(Exodus 15:22-27)

God has saved the firstborn Hebrews, sent plagues upon Egypt, and delivered all the Hebrews from bondage. The Hebrews were trapped between the Red Sea and the approaching Egyptian soldiers and forgot all that God had done to secure their freedom and began to murmur. Again, God displays His power and love for the Hebrews and splits the Red Sea to allow them to cross over safely. Just in case someone would rise to say that the Red Sea was low in that area or at that time of year, God released the waters and drowned all the Egyptian soldiers in that part of the Red Sea.

After these great miracles and displays of love and power, the Hebrews still had doubts that God would see them through and complained about their lack of clean drinking water. Some of us are the same way today, having seen all that God has done to call us to His service and secure our freedom from bondage. We look for empirical evidence that God exists and that God is with us instead of living by faith. The Hebrews were living by their senses instead of by their faith in God.

Before the Hebrews arrived at Marah, they roamed the wilderness without water for three days, so they thought they were relieved of thirst when they found water. However, the water was not drinkable. The water was too bitter and made them crave clean water to wash down the bitter water. It was at this time that they complained to Moses. They spoke among themselves and blamed Moses for every perceived setback. These were viewed as setbacks because the Hebrews were not living by faith and trusting in God. They believed their flesh, and their flesh told them that they were thirsty and there was no drinkable water in sight.

In today's world, we do the same. We go through severe trials, and we endure and persevere. However, instead of drawing on those experiences, learning from them, and remembering how we persevered, we often feel powerless and overwhelmed, filling our minds with negativity.

As a social worker, I can help people realize that they have built up resilience by going through past trials, and they can get through future tests as well. As a minister, I can help people understand that God has brought them through too many trials for them to give up. The Hebrews in the wilderness did not realize how resilient their ancestors were, having endured over four hundred years of slavery, and how they had endured trials since leaving Egypt. Throughout their history, God has been with them and has not called them into the wilderness to let them die. Of course, I benefit from reading the Bible, and I know how the story turns out.

If you wonder how you will get through a trial, just remember when you were in crisis and how you endured and persevered. Draw on that experience and prepare yourself to get through your next crisis. As Christians, we need to remember how far God has brought us and walk in faith with the resilience we have built up over the years.

In Verse 25, Moses cries out to God. Moses continuously depends on God, and now there is another crisis. Moses cried out as a minister to the Hebrews. Moses was not a tour guide. He was not called merely to guide the Hebrews through the wilderness. He ministered to God's people, and he was concerned about their spiritual well-being.

Moses trusted in God and believed that God would supply water, but Moses also knew that some of the Hebrew's faith was fragile, and he did not want to lose anyone who could not endure another trial. Even when a minister trusts in God and knows that all is in God's will, the minister still hurts with the person in crisis and cries out to God.

As ministers, we may struggle with faith issues when we depend on God to resolve the problems of those we are called to serve, yet they continue to hurt. As ministers, we need to be ministered to as well, and our faith is stronger when we see them exercising their faith in the face of trials. Ministry works both ways. A pastor can encourage the flock to stand on faith and depend on God, and the greatest reward is when the congregation puts the pastor's teachings into practice and perseveres through trials. That is how the group can minister to the pastor or minister.

Although Moses depended on God, he longed to see the Hebrews trust in God. That is why Moses cried out to God on behalf of the Hebrews. It was not that Moses' faith was weak; it was that he was hurting with God's people. God answered Moses' cries and supplied drinkable water to the Hebrews in the wilderness.

God knows our situations and changes what is bitter into something sweet if we persevere by faith. Extreme bondage turned into sweet freedom, bitter water turned into fresh water, and painful experiences on earth will be turned into sweet Glory in Heaven if we endure the suffering and allow God to prepare us for Glory.

2

Humbled by Discipline

God uses discipline to humble us. In this chapter, we will study the Book of Deuteronomy and see how God waited for the Hebrews to be ready for the Promised Land.

God would not bless them one moment before they were prepared. God had to see humility in them to know that they will remember how God sustained them in the wilderness and that they will not forget God when they prospered.

In Deuteronomy, we see that the generation that had been delivered from Egypt and saw so many of God's miracles in the wilderness was gone, and the new generation was poised to enter the Promised Land. This new nation was humbled and matured during the years of wandering in the desert.

Deuteronomy 4:4 tells us that this generation ***"held fast to the Lord."*** Moses realizes that he will not live long enough to enter the Promised Land with the Hebrews and assembles them to review and give another sermon on living holy. Deuteronomy is a book of sermons from Moses to God's people and leads the Hebrews much like our church leaders lead us into a better way of serving and honoring God through the sermons that they deliver.

In chapter eight of Deuteronomy, the author uses the forty years in the wilderness and God's compassionate guidance and instruction of the Hebrew people to illustrate five points:

1. The Hebrew people are to be obedient to God. The Hebrews took forty years to grasp the concept of obedience to God's precepts. It was time that obedience became an integral part of the relationship between the Hebrews and God.
2. The Hebrew people had a short memory and forgot God's miracles to sustain them in the wilderness.
3. The Hebrew people needed to know that the Promised Land was worth the wait and that obedience would make their stay in the desert more satisfying and abundant.
4. The Hebrew people needed to learn that being obedient and humble would help them keep their new blessings in perspective, so they will not go astray when they prosper.
5. The Hebrew people needed to know the consequences of abandoning their loyalty and obedience to God.

These five points were meant to remind the Hebrews of the humbling experiences that God allowed them to suffer in the wilderness.

> ***8*** *This entire commandment that I command you today you must diligently observe, so that you may live and increase, and go in and occupy the land that the LORD promised on oath to your ancestors.* [2] *Remember the long way that the LORD, your God, has led you these forty years in the wilderness, in order to humble you, testing you to know what was in your heart, whether or not you would keep his commandments.* [3] *He humbled you by letting you hunger, then by feeding you with manna, with which neither you nor your ancestors were acquainted, to make you understand that one does not live by bread alone but by every word that comes from the mouth of the LORD.* [4] *The clothes on your back did not wear out. Your feet did not swell these forty years.* [5] *Know then in your heart that as a parent disciplines a child, so the LORD your God disciplines you.* [6] *Therefore, keep the Lord your God's commandments by walking in his ways and by fearing him.* [7] *For the LORD your God is bringing you into a good land, a land with flowing streams, with springs and underground waters welling up in valleys and hills,* [8]*a land of wheat and barley, of vines and fig trees and pomegranates, an area of olive trees and honey,* [9] *a land where you may eat bread without scarcity, where you will lack nothing, a nation whose stones are iron and from whose hills you may mine copper.* [10] *You shall eat your fill and bless the LORD your God for the good land he has given you.* **(Deuteronomy 8:1-10)**

Before we can enter God's Glory, we must rid ourselves of self-righteousness, pride, and worldly desires. We must be humbled to appreciate God's blessings and not act as if we are entitled to God's blessings. In Deuteronomy chapter 8, God explains to the Hebrew people that the time spent in the wilderness should not be forgotten. It is essential to know the reason for the time spent in the desert. The time spent in the desert was a form of discipline at God's will. God used discipline to prepare the Hebrews to receive God's blessings.

Before God can bless us, we must be able to appreciate and do well with His blessings. God must be able to trust us with His blessings. The Hebrew people had to learn to trust in God's promises so that when they entered the Promised Land, they would not forget how they got there. In this chapter, God teaches them that they are to submit to and fear the God who loves them enough to discipline them and instruct them in the paths they should follow. It did not take God forty years to train them, but it took forty years for the Hebrews to shed their pride and carnal desires and prepare for Glory. We can see God doing the same with us today. Bible study is so much fun; what God taught thousands of years ago is taught today. God is the same today as thousands of years ago. Sadly, so are we.

1) The Hebrew people are to be obedient to God. The Hebrews took forty years to grasp the concept of obedience to God's precepts. It was time that obedience became an integral part of the relationship between the Hebrews and God.

The Hebrews are taken out of bondage and disciplined in the wilderness so that God can trust them with His Glory. As Christians, we are called out of the bondage of sin and worldly desires and disciplined so that we may be humbled and appreciate God. All too many times, we murmur at our disciplines instead of being patient and letting God bless us.

2) The Hebrew people forgot the miracles that God used to sustain them in the wilderness.

As Christians, we also must remember where God has delivered us from and stop complaining when we think God has abandoned us during our suffering. Then, we are humbled when God delivers us again.

3) The Hebrews needed to know that the Promised Land was worth the wait and that obedience would make their stay in this land more satisfying and abundant.

As Christians, we can be delivered from tragic events. Sometimes, we still do not understand that we need to obey the rules to enjoy existence without facing similar catastrophic circumstances.

4) Being obedient and humble would help the Hebrews keep their new blessings in perspective, so they will not go astray when they prosper.

God is always looking to bless the person set apart from the world for a higher purpose. Can you handle what God has in store for you?

5) The Hebrew people needed to know the consequences of abandoning their loyalty and obedience to God.

As God's people, it would be in our best interest to know that we may regress into sin if we abandon our loyalty and obedience to God. Some of us never recover.

This chapter of Deuteronomy reminds us that trials can cause us to depend on God and that prosperity can cause us to forget about God. The key is to remember where we were in our misery, not forget God when all is well. God teaches us lessons through discipline and mercy. Once God trains us, we can appreciate His blessings.

3

The Severe Trials of the Godly

When people are living a life contrary to what the Bible refers to as "godly living," it is easy for us to justify their suffering or trials. We usually say that their troubles were severe because of their godlessness. But what is our response when those who are living Godly lives suffer afflictions? In the first verse of the Book of Job, the author states that Job was blameless and upright, confirmed by God in the eighth verse.

Job and His Family

There was once a man in the land of Uz, whose name was Job. That man was blameless and upright, one who feared God and turned away from evil. [2] There were born to him seven sons and three daughters. [3] He had seven thousand sheep, three thousand camels, five hundred yoke of oxen, five hundred donkeys, and very many servants; so that this man was the greatest of all the people of the east. [4] His sons used to go and hold feasts in one another's houses in turn, and they would send and invite their three sisters to eat and drink with them. [5] And when the feast days had run their course, Job would send and sanctify them, and he would rise early in the morning and offer burnt offerings according to the number of them all; for Job said, "It may be that my children have sinned, and cursed God in their hearts." This is what Job always did. **(Job1:1-5)**

Attack on Job's Character

[6] *One day, the heavenly beings came to present themselves before the LORD, and Satan also came among them.* [7] *The LORD said to Satan, "Where have you come from?" Satan answered the LORD, "From going to and fro on the earth, and from walking up and down on it."* [8] *The LORD said to Satan, "Have you considered my servant Job? There is no one like him on the earth, a blameless and upright man who fears God and turns away from evil."* [9] *Then Satan answered the LORD, "Does Job fear God for nothing?* [10]*Have you not put a fence around him and his house and all that he has on every side? You have blessed the work of his hands, and his possessions have increased in the land.* [11] *But stretch out your hand now and touch all that he has, and he will curse you to your face."* [12] *The LORD said to Satan, "Very well, all that he has is in your power; only do not stretch out your hand against him!" So, Satan went out from the presence of the LORD.* **(Job 1:6-12)**

There are times when angels come before God to give an account to God of their works here on earth and how they completed their earlier instructions. God knows whether they complete their tasks or not and probably meets with them to commend them and give them further instructions. In this case, God knew that Satan had entered the meeting uninvited and knew that Satan came with ill intentions. No matter how evil the plans, Satan can never afflict us unless: (a) we purposefully look to do evil, and if we do, we are in Satan's will, or (b) God allows Satan to afflict us. God has restricted Satan from doing us harm without permission.

At this point, God speaks highly of Job. God speaking highly of Job must have infuriated Satan because Satan says that Job aligns himself with God because it is convenient. To dispel Satan's character assassination of Job, God allows Satan to strip Job of all his possessions but does not allow Satan to harm his body.

There are clear boundaries that Satan cannot cross when it comes to our welfare. No matter what afflictions and trials come upon us, we will not suffer beyond what we need to make us stronger on our journey toward eternity with God. To some, it may be disheartening to imagine that God will strip us of all our worldly blessings, but when we look at things through godly lenses, we realize that we have anything only because God allows us to, and God retains the right to take it all away. We must not pay too much attention to good times or tough times, which last for just a season. Let us master our experiences and honor God for better or for worse.

> [20] *Then Job arose, tore his robe, shaved his head, and fell*
> *on the ground, and worshiped.* [21] *He said, "Naked I came*

> *from my mother's womb, and naked shall I return there; the LORD gave, and the LORD has taken away; blessed be the name of the LORD."* [22]*In all this, Job did not sin or charge God with wrongdoing.*
> **(Job 1:20-22)**

What is your reason for your faith and service to God? If it is merely for the blessings of God, your faith may waver as soon as adversity enters your life. Satan was sure that Job served God only because God had blessed him. Satan was wrong, just as God predicted. How will you fare when afflictions and trials become part of your life? Will your faith waver? Will you curse God? Do not stress. God doesn't hold us to the same standards as Job. Let us try not to take so many stories in the Bible so literally, and let us focus on the lessons that we can learn from the information. We will lose our minds if we try to be exactly like the people in the Bible.

When we suffer afflictions and trials, we hurt, cry, shout, place blame, curse, and might indulge in maladaptive coping mechanisms (e.g., alcohol, drugs, sexual promiscuity, etc.). We are human, so we act human. Christ's humanity cried out to God from the cross when it seemed that God had abandoned Him, so we should stop trying to be so heroic and realize that we have weaknesses as humans. It is how we deal with these weaknesses that matter. Do we fold in the face of adversity, or do we rely on our spiritual resilience built in us by God through past difficulties?

Job, the wealthiest man in the East, was now destitute and alone, yet he remained where he was before his afflictions in the presence of God. Job recognized that he was born naked with no money, children, or wife. He only had anything because God gave to him what God saw fit to give to him. Now, God had chosen to allow these earthly amenities and relationships to decrease, but Job's religion did not decline. That was something that Job had to give up freely, and according to the story, Job never gave that up.

He lost everything except his love for and faith in God. We can never lose our salvation, but we can give it up if we take our minds off God and God's sovereignty. No matter how naked and destitute we may be, we can never be more exposed and vulnerable than we were at the time of our birth. God provided for us then and will continue to provide for us. In all our sufferings, it will serve us well not to sin or charge God with wrongdoing. Patience allowed Job to die of old age and not of sorrows and afflictions.

Attack on Job's Health

1 One day, the heavenly beings came to present themselves before the LORD, and Satan also came among them to present himself before the LORD. 2 The LORD said to Satan, "Where have you come from?" Satan answered the

LORD, "From going to and fro on the earth, and from walking up and down on it." 3 The LORD said to Satan, "Have you considered my servant Job? There is no one like him on the earth, a blameless and upright man who fears God and turns away from evil. He persists in his integrity, although you incited me against him, to destroy him for no reason." 4 Then Satan answered the LORD, "Skin for skin! All that people have, they will give to save their lives. 5 But stretch out your hand now and touch his bone and his flesh, and he will curse you to your face." 6 The LORD said to Satan, "Very well, he is in your power; only spare his life." 7 So Satan went out from the presence of the LORD and inflicted loathsome sores on Job from the sole of his foot to the crown of his head. 8Job took a potsherd with which to scrape himself and sat among the ashes. **(Job 2:1-10)**

Job's Wife

9 Then his wife said to him, "Do you persist in your integrity? Curse God and die." 10 But, he said to her, "You speak as any foolish woman would speak. Shall we receive the good at the hand of God and not receive the bad?" In all this, Job did not sin with his lips.
(Job 2:9-10)

These two verses are all that we know about Job's wife. She is well known by many who have read the Book of Job or have heard of a sermon on the Book. She is vilified as a faithless, disrespectful, and sinful woman because she cries for Job to curse God. Some may say that Satan had used her to have Job do what

Satan could not make Job do, which was to curse God. Satan was the one who asked God for permission to attack Job and said to God that "he (Job) will curse you to your face." Had Mrs. Job lost all hope in her God that she opted to consult with Satan about her husband's suffering? Maybe while she was conversing with Satan, she found out that Job had to curse God to end the pain. We are insensitive when we pass such harsh judgment on this woman of God.

Let us go back to the beginning of the Book of Job, where the author describes the prosperity of Job. He is a man of great wealth and seven sons and three daughters. That leads me to believe that there may have been a woman in Job's life. The author does not describe Job as a widower or a lonely man, so it may be fair to think that Job had a wife. Since God describes him as a blameless and upright man and a pious man, I understand Job as a man of God who spent time in the temple and offered sacrifices to God. The wife of a prosperous and godly man is usually a faithful, strong, and godly woman. A family as wealthy as this family needs the benefit of both a husband/father and a wife/mother. We only get two sentences from this godly woman, and she is rebuked by Job and told that she "speaks as any foolish woman." We can learn a lot from the brief appearance of this godly woman.

When Job lost his children, so did she. When Job lost his wealth, so did she, but she did not speak up probably because she was a woman who knew God as a loving God of justice, and she knew her husband well enough to know that he was faithful and upright and God would sustain Job. She lived in a world where the righteous were blessed, and the unrighteous were cursed, and righteousness must prevail. Mrs. Job was hurting just as much as Job, if not more, but she kept silent. Then she sees her husband's health afflicted, and now she is pushed out to the limit of her faith. My heart aches for her. She has suffered so much loss, yet she has not spoken a word against God, nor has she accused Job of any wrong. Is her comment to Job a sign of weakness? I think not. I see her as a woman who dares to question the devastation that she is experiencing. She is still a woman of God; only she now needs to assign meaning to the suffering. God must have a reason for all of Job's pain, and since she could not see her loving husband suffer any longer, she says what she believes is Job's only way out, and that is to curse God and die.

She was not a weak woman, as far as I can understand. She was a woman grappling with a situation that defied all that she knew about her faith tradition. She was a woman who was trying to understand her world and grow in faith. She had to verbalize what she was feeling to grow in strength and hope. We give God our undivided attention when we question our reasons to press on when it appears that God has abandoned us. Questioning God can help us grow in faith, and it was necessary for Job's wife in this story.

Job's Three Friends

> [11] *Now, when Job's three friends heard of all these troubles that had come upon him, each of them sets out from his home—Eliphaz the Temanite, Bildad the Shuhite, and Zophar the Naamathite. They met to go and console and comfort him.* [12] *When they saw him from a distance, they did not recognize him, and they raised their voices and wept aloud; they tore their robes and threw dust in the air upon their heads.* [13] *They sat with him on the ground seven days and seven nights, and no one spoke a word to him, for they saw that his suffering was very great.*
> **(Job 2:11-13)**

Job's friends came and sat with him for seven days and nights without uttering a word of judgment. They cried aloud and tore their robes and threw dust on their heads like Job and shared in his humility. Because these friends came to comfort Job in his suffering, it can be fair to say that they were close when Job was healthy and prosperous; only the sincere are around to comfort us in times of despair. Some delight in our suffering, but they come only to confirm our pain and quickly run to spread the word. Eliphaz, Bildad, and Zophar sat with Job in silence, trying to understand why a righteous man who honored and feared God was suffering.

Then Job was the first to speak, cursing the day he was born. We have often heard of the patience of Job, so you may have been disillusioned to know that Job cursed the day that he was born. Not knowing the reasons for his suffering caused Job to curse the day that he was born. Why would a godly man suffer in such a way? Well, let us not lose our focus on why Job was suffering. Satan said that Job would curse God during his suffering, and Job never cursed God.

As a man, Job expressed a desire not to suffer any longer, and since he did not know the source of his suffering, he wished that he was never born. Job's friends questioned whether Job was indeed an honest and honorable man or merely a hypocrite. Job's friends began to comment on the possible reasons for Job's suffering.

It's incomprehensible to us that God would let the godly suffer. Hence, we want to intellectualize the pain by believing that although a person may appear to be godly, they must have done something wrong to incur the wrath of God. Why do we think that way? Well, if we know a person who is godly and avoids even the appearance of evil, we expect them to be prosperous and blessed. However, if we see that same person suffer trials, we must believe that there is a reason for their suffering to qualify God's justice.

We equate blessings with godliness and afflictions with sinfulness. The pain must be a consequence of sin because if the godly can suffer hardships, then we who are less pious are in serious trouble.

Let us understand Job's three friends, Eliphaz from Teman, Bildad from Shuah, and Zophar from Naamath, and their comments to Job regarding his afflictions. The first verses of the Book of Job describe Job's prosperity and righteousness, known by all the community members, especially his friends. It would be fair to say that Job's friends were fearful that if a blameless and upright man could suffer such afflictions, then either God was unjust or Job somehow fell out of God's favor. If a man as pious as Job could suffer hardships, they were really in trouble because there was no one in the land as godly as Job. Not wanting to believe that God was unjust, they turned their attention to Job.

We feel the need to assign meaning to all we experience, or life will appear to have no purpose. Whether we suffer afflictions because of our sin or not should not be our focus. Our focus should be on how trials and hardships can bring us closer to God and make us better people, thus preparing us for Glory.

4

Afflictions Teach Us God's Precepts

Afflictions tend to humble the prideful person. Why would we become prideful and need to be humbled? Prosperity can cause us to take our minds off God's statutes (laws). As children, we are praised when we do well. We want to receive praise instead of offering praise. A wise person will realize that to overcome afflictions, he must change his ways to improve the results.

In Charles Dickens' "A Christmas Carol," first published on December 19, 1843, in London, England, by Chapman and Hall, Ebenezer Scrooge is fearful that he cannot change the inevitable fate because of the way he lives his life. He says to the Ghost of Christmas Yet to Come, "Men's courses will foreshadow certain ends, to which, if persevered in, they must lead."

"But if the courses are departed from, the ends will change. Say it is thus with what you show me." It can be fair to say that the Ghost of Christmas Yet to Come signifies our fears of the future and our control over it. Life is what we make of it. Scrooge became wise when he realized that he could change his afflictions by changing his ways, and so it is when we suffer hardships because of our habits. We can change our fate if we allow afflictions to humble us. A fool is one who keeps his pride during misfortune and refuses to humble himself before God.

Psalm 119
A Celebration of God's Word

This Psalm is an Acrostic Psalm (i.e., it follows an alphabetical arrangement of the original Hebrew language). There are many terms in this Psalm that refer to the Word of God. These are:

- Torah, found 25 times, is the complete body of teachings found in the Hebrew Bible's first five books.
- Commandments found 21 times are precise, specific directives issued by God.
- Decrees found 23 times referring to things written and established in the law.
- Judgments found 19 times, indicating a binding judicial decision establishing a precedent.
- Precepts found 21 times in poetry and are synonymous with edicts.

- Statutes found 23 times are a profound expression of God's standards for human behavior.
- Word found 27 times refers to the laws given to the Israelites by God through Moses.
- Sayings found 19 times and are synonymous with Word.
- Way found 25 times. The ways of God.

In this Psalm, the Psalmist expresses the joy found in scripture. The Psalmist calls scripture "The Word of Truth." To say that scripture is the truth means that it can be trusted completely, penetrating all man's illusions while portraying reality as God intended.

> *"67 Before I was humbled, I went astray, but now I keep your word.*
> **(Psalm 119:67-68)**

When we get too fond of ourselves, we submit to the desires of our flesh. We think that we can overcome all situations because we are more significant than life. Prosperity tends to give us a false sense of security, and it is at these times that we need to be afflicted so that we may hear God more clearly. We are physically afflicted before we cause ourselves to be spiritually afflicted. When we go astray, we choose to walk among others outside of the will of God. Afflictions are God's way of redirecting us back onto the proper path.

The Psalmist is testifying to us so that we may refrain from falling into prideful thinking and foolish actions that bring about a dreadful consequence (i.e., eternal separation from God). When we go astray or sin, the resulting affliction is a way for us to learn how it was that we went wrong so that we may be able to identify the signs and symptoms to prevent it from happening again.

As a psychotherapist, I have treated substance abusers, and one of the first things I want my clients to understand is that relapses are part of recovery. A large percentage of all the people who come into treatment for substance abuse or dependence will relapse, which can be very disheartening to someone who wants to stop using substances. However, if the client keeps a daily journal of the days following the first day that they decided to stop using drugs, they can see signs and symptoms that present themselves before a relapse. Getting to know these signs and symptoms can help them avoid the triggers that can send them back into the whirlwind of addiction. It is similar to when a person decides to walk in the ways of God and forsake sin. When we fall into sin and go astray from the statutes of God, afflictions can help us realize that we are going back into the whirlwind of sinful desires.

If we suffer hardships but refuse to learn about the signs that brought the miseries upon us, we are destined to remain afflicted until we know how to stay humble without having to be afflicted so that we may be humbled.

"68You are good and do good. Teach me your statutes."

When we realize that God will allow affliction so that we may mature spiritually, we can recognize that affliction is a way God uses to correct us and point us in the right direction. This direction will lead us to seek God's statutes (laws). The Psalmist is thankful that God loves him enough to afflict him. The Psalmist recognizes that afflictions allowed by God will lead to his purification. Therefore, God is good and does good consistently. It is hard to look on the bright side of affliction while we are amid the pain, but the Psalmist takes a moment in this Psalm to praise God. Hardships have a defining quality that can bring us to a spiritual maturity that prepares us to receive God's statutes.

Afflictions bring us to our knees to seek God's grace, be led by God's laws, and live good lives with good intentions. Sufferings allowed by God are the best that we can hope for when we go astray if we realize that all things that come from God have a useful purpose. Anything that brings us closer to God and causes us to crave God's guidance is good for us, and the Psalmist shares that with us in Psalm 119:67-68.

71 It is suitable for me that I was humbled.
So that I might learn your statutes.

(Psalms 119:71-72)

Afflictions lead to our knowledge and the grace of God. Do not be surprised if you suffer more afflictions the closer you come to following God's statutes. We can never be too prepared to stand in the presence of God. The Psalmist was close to God but afflicted. It is to our advantage to be afflicted because there is much to be learned through afflictions.

> *"72 The law of your mouth is better for me. Than thousands of gold and silver pieces."*

Learning God's laws is worth more to us than any number of precious metals. Afflictions should direct us to God's Word. The Psalmist had only a fraction of the Word of God, yet most of us value God's Word only a fraction of how much the Psalmist valued God's Word.

I have often wondered what my life would have been like if I were born wealthy or acquired wealth. I would be able to get more goods and services than I can afford today, but that will not alleviate my afflictions. However, the pain has led me to God's Word, and God's Word has helped me deal with my suffering by getting closer to God and understanding God's purpose for my life. When we are afflicted, we have an opportunity to reflect on our lives. We have a chance to reflect on the past and present of our physical and spiritual existence. At that point, a person with a sincere and contrite heart realizes that they need to learn more about God's laws. Humbled by affliction, the Psalmist realizes that no earthly riches can compare to the spiritual means that God has for him if he submits to God's statutes.

> [75] *I know, O LORD, that your judgments are right and that in faithfulness, you have humbled me.*
> **(Psalm 119:75-76)**

It is difficult to rejoice in anything that brings us sorrow, but the Psalmist takes pleasure in realizing that his affliction is a judgment handed down to him from God. No matter the reason for our misery, whether a punishment from God or righteous suffering, one thing remains constant. The distress allows us to be humbled before God and receive God's instructions on being a greater witness of God's righteousness in the world.

Although we hurt, we can take comfort in understanding that God is faithful and is pleased if our pain helps us understand humility and the role that adversity plays in softening our hardened hearts and humbling our prideful personalities. We can view suffering as a form of discipline that is meant to correct us when we go astray, as the Psalmist realizes in this Psalm. When we see suffering this way, we understand that we are disciplined by those who love us.

If we do not learn to follow rules and laws, then the government will separate us from society to protect society from our foolish and unlawful actions. The Psalmist realizes that he has broken God's laws and does not want to suffer affliction in vain. The Psalmist asks God to take this time to fill his heart with the laws that will set him on the path to godliness. This path leads to physical and spiritual victory on earth and in the afterlife.

"[76] Let your steadfast love become my comfort."

If we suffer afflictions for no reason and with no hope of an end to the pain, we as human beings may become angry and hateful. If we believe in a faithful and righteous God, we can persevere through all types of hardships, knowing that God will never abandon us. While we are still in our afflictions, we can remain faithful that our God will comfort us. We must practice honest faith. A sincere faith is one that understands that afflictions will lead to a better understanding of God's laws and God's will for our lives while praying for redemption and comfort. We are not numb to pain and sorrows. We would rather not experience pain, so it's ok to ask God for support while being purified and prepared for glory.

Afflictions prepare us for God's glory, not our glory. Do not feel less godly if you want to be comforted through your pain because this is the nature of all creatures that roam the earth. It is in our nature to seek comfort instead of suffering. Just realize that the only support that can genuinely relieve our pain comes from God, as the Psalmist recognizes in this Psalm.

5

Even a King Praises God for Discipline

King Hezekiah

[9]A writing of King Hezekiah of Judah, after he had been sick and had recovered from his sickness: [10] I said: In the noontide of my days I must depart; I am consigned to the gates of Sheol for the rest of my years.[11]I said, I shall not see the LORD in the land of the living; I shall look upon mortals no more among the inhabitants of the world.[12]My dwelling is plucked up and removed from me like a shepherd's tent; like a weaver, I have rolled up my life; he cuts me off from the loom; from day to night you bring me to an end; [13]I cry for help until morning; like a lion, he breaks all my bones; from day to night you bring me to an end. [14] Like a swallow or a crane, I clamor; I moan like a dove. My eyes are weary while looking upward. O Lord, I am oppressed; be my security! [15] But what can I say? For he has spoken to me, and he has done it. All my sleep has fled because of the bitterness of my soul. [16]O Lord, by these things people live, and in all these is the life of my spirit. Oh, restore me to health and make me live! [17]Surely it was

for my welfare that I had great bitterness, but you have held back my life from the pit of destruction, for you have cast all my sins behind your back. [18] *For Sheol cannot thank you; death cannot praise you; those who go down to the Pit cannot hope for your faithfulness.* [19] *The living, the living, they thank you, as I do this day; fathers make known to children your faithfulness.* [20] *The LORD will save me, and we will sing to stringed instruments all the days of our lives, at the house of the LORD.*
(Isaiah 38:9-20)

King Hezekiah wrote a Thanksgiving Song after his deliverance from illness. It was a divine inspiration written down to remind him when he was so ill that total reliance on God was the only way to overcome his situation. He also wanted his subjects to know how they could overcome similar problems.

We often keep journals to keep track of events in our lives and how we dealt with certain situations to reference them in similar circumstances. King Hezekiah is so grateful for his deliverance; he wanted to be reminded of it as often as possible. It also serves as a reminder not to repeat the same behaviors that cause pain. Hezekiah reminds himself of the condition he was in while he was ill ***(v10-13)***. He writes about his negative thoughts of himself while he was at his worst. Hezekiah blamed himself for his condition and gave up on himself. He also wanted to remind himself of a time when he thought death was imminent and wanted to magnify the power of God after his restoration.

Hezekiah reminds himself of how he complained about his condition and lost trust in God. He was ashamed of his complaining in prayer, but God still honored his prayers. Hezekiah acknowledged God's grace after his recovery. While Isaiah was telling him that he would recover and live 15 more years, Hezekiah believed it as if it had already happened. He had trusted in his recovery before he had recovered.

We can learn to trust in God before and not only after our deliverance. Therefore, Hezekiah promises himself never to forget the way he complained when he was afflicted. He sets out to encourage others to rely on God because God will not disappoint them. God gives hope in hopeless situations. The more God shows us love and mercy in our afflictions, the more we should rely on God.

Discipline and Sanctification

God's discipline is intended to separate Christians from sinful behaviors, desires, and characters of those who choose not to believe in the Anointed One (Christ). This separation from those things that are unholy or distract Christians from their work in Christ is sanctification. As Christians, we are to be set apart from carnal desires and made available for the service of our Lord and Savior, Jesus Christ. The process by which this sanctification begins is through discipline. The New Testament refers to the verb "to sanctify" in several verses. We will explore a few in this chapter.

> [17]*You blind fools! For which is more significant, the gold or the sanctuary that has made the gold sacred?* [18] *And you say, 'Whoever swears by the altar is bound by nothing, but whoever swears by the gift that is on the altar is bound by the oath.'* [19] *How blind you are! For which is more excellent, the gift or the altar that makes the gift sacred?*
> **(Matthew 23:17-19)**

In Chapter 23 of the Gospel of Matthew, Jesus denounces the Scribes and Pharisees because they sought their worldly gain and honor before they sought God's glory. He distinguished earthly riches and godly riches when He asked the Scribes and Pharisees if the temple's gold was more significant than the temple. In the minds of the Scribes and Pharisees, gold gifts made the temple valuable. They thought this because their focus was on economic value and not spiritual significance. Jesus was explaining to them that the temple was what increased the value of the gold. Jesus was not saying that gold had no value; he was distinguishing the value of gold and the value of the temple. The most valuable is the temple, and gold increases in value when it is in the temple. The gold on the altar of the temple was set apart or sanctified for the Lord and had more value. The gold inside of the temple serves a higher purpose.

As human beings, we all have value, but when sanctified for the service of our Lord and Savior Jesus Christ, we serve a higher purpose and, therefore, are worth more to this world. This sanctification occurs when we accept and endure God's discipline to enhance our spiritual worth on earth.

Hebrews 12:5-11

In Chapter 12 of the Book of Hebrews, the author explains how struggles strengthen and purify Christians. The author also explains that some afflictions to Christians come because of God's discipline to promote sanctification. We need faith when we face situations intended to discipline us. We can use Christ as an example of how to endure suffering and persecution and persevere until death.

Good parents discipline their children to separate them from foolish behaviors that may bring them anguish in the future. God also disciplines us to keep us from irrational and unbridled carnal behavior. God's discipline is wiser and leads us to more excellent ends. So, we continue through our struggles with courage and hope. The hope is that God's discipline will create a healthier and more faithful Christian. God's training is a hardship, but this discipline is divine and is a responsibility of God. Many people view God's training as an expression of anger. God's discipline is an expression of love intended to lead us to holiness. All punishment should be for the good of those who are disciplined.

> [5] *And you have forgotten the exhortation that addresses you as children— "My child, do not regard lightly the discipline of the Lord, or lose heart when he punishes you;*
> [6] *for the Lord disciplines those whom he loves, and chastises every child whom he accepts.*
> **(Hebrews 12:5-6)**

In verse five, the author of Hebrews explains that although it may seem that our suffering may come from the world around us, God plays the ultimate role in our affliction so that we are disciplined. Therefore, our sorrows are the parental chastisements of God. As Christians, we are instructed not to do certain things while enduring pain. We must not be angered by our suffering or charge God with any wrong. As human beings, it is difficult not to express emotions, but in this verse, the author reminds us that it will benefit us if we endure God's discipline. It takes great control to hold our emotions and focus on how we can benefit from our suffering. We must not minimize our sorrow, or we will be minimizing God and the purpose of our pain. We must not go astray during our grief. We must not fear the misfortunes that touch our lives because of God's discipline. We must stand in faith and look for God's blessing.

Parents who discipline their children out of love do not abort the disciplinary actions at the request of the child. Parents who genuinely love their children let the discipline continue until a lesson is learned. We can be sure that we have been or will be disciplined by God at some point in our lives because we can never be perfect. No one can escape the disciplinary actions of God. Therefore, we should look forward to God's disciplinary actions because it is inevitable. There is nowhere to hide from God's love. Discipline is a gift of love from God.

We often wonder why the godless never seem to suffer as much as the godly, and there is a good reason for that. As children of God, we are disciplined by God more often and more severely. As a teenager, I was punished by my mother, and I found myself wishing that she would let me live as my friend's parents let them live. Over 50 years later, those friends are dead, imprisoned, still on the streets of Chicago, or addicted to drugs and or alcohol. I was able to leave the street life because I was disciplined and given rules to follow, and I endured the discipline and made an honest effort to follow the rules. It is the same for God's children. We are not allowed to run wild and unsupervised because God is the ultimate loving parent.

I am not saying that all the people who suffer consequences were forsaken by their parents. Discipline works both ways. It must be provided and received. If provided by the parent but not accepted by the child, it's as if it was never provided at all. We must rejoice when God disciplines us, for God's discipline is justice.

> [13] *For suppose the blood of goats and bulls, with the sprinkling of the ashes of a heifer, sanctifies those who have been defiled so that their flesh is purified. In that case,*
> [14] *how much more will the blood of Christ, who through the eternal Spirit offered himself without blemish to God, purify our conscience from dead works to worship the living God!*
> **(Hebrews 9:13-14)**

As Christians called to holiness, we are to be pure and blameless to serve the world as God intended. But how can we be pure and innocent in a world full of sinful opportunities while we have an opportunistic flesh that is always seeking a chance to satisfy its desires? We can understand this better if we know the cleaning rituals of the Hebrews. Knowing that they were impure, they sought from God a way to be set apart from the impurities of the world around them. God answered the Hebrews by requiring the sacrifice of a perfect heifer and the sprinkling of the ashes of the heifer on those who were to be set apart or sanctified to serve God, an external sanctification process.

In Christ, we have a new sanctification process, internal sanctification. Only the blood of a holy, perfect human being would be able to meet the requirements of God's purification process. There was no such human being on all the earth, so God sent us a living being that was 100% God in heaven and 100% human on earth. Christ became flesh for the purification of our souls and the sanctification of our lives. Christ offered up His pure and perfect body as a sacrifice so that His blood would clean us of our impurities and set us apart or sanctify us for His purpose. His purpose is more excellent than ours. God uses discipline to put and keep us on track. Discipline prepares us for God's glory.

The Book of Hebrews compares the Old Testament revelation as the prediction of Christ and The New Testament as the revelation of Christ. Angels brought the Old Testament revelation, while the Son of God brought the New Testament revelation. The title (Hebrews) tells us that this book was intended for the Jewish community, recently converted Jewish Christians who may have felt drawn back to their Judaic traditions. These traditions required repetitive sacrifices to atone for the sins of the Hebrews, but Christ offered His life to atone for all the sins of the world. Christ paid the eternal salvation for the world with one act of love.

The author of Hebrews advocates teaching Christianity to a Hebrew community that loved and revered their traditions. These traditions were rooted in the Old Testament and were good, but the author of the Book of Hebrews authored this book to enlighten the

Hebrew community about the New Testament. The New Testament fulfills the promises made in the Old Testament. The Hebrew community was familiar with the signs of the Old Testament. The author of the Book of Hebrews offered his writings to explain how the New Testament fulfills those promises.

Jesus Christ was a practicing Hebrew. He was a good first-century Jewish man who observed all the traditions and revelations that the angels brought with the Old Testament. The Book of Hebrews respects Old Testament traditions. The author of Hebrews explains to this community how the Old Testament points us in the direction of Christ and the New Testament. If a person wants to follow the precepts of Christ, an excellent place to start is in the Old Testament. We can learn a lot about discipline and sanctification by studying the Old Testament. As a seminary student, I completed a course on Judaism that helped me appreciate how Christ remained disciplined and sanctified through all the trials and persecutions that He endured.

The fruits of discipline are worth the pain. Living through corrective training is not easy. Nowhere in the Bible will you read that aligning yourself with God and humbly submitting to God's discipline is easy. Yet, God calls us to be humble and submissive when we are disciplined. As human beings, we are the most stubborn of all of God's creatures. We will continue to seek those things that our flesh desires regardless of the consequences. When we are disciplined because our actions are harmful to us or others, we fight against the disciplinarian and discipline. Discipline is tough enough to endure without being rebellious against the disciplinarian. Yet, as human beings, we choose to add to our affliction by taking a stubborn stance against the one who disciplines us for our good and the good of our community.

Let us compare human stubbornness to that of God's other creatures. When other animals want something, they will abandon the behavior if they feel pain. God sets out to teach us valuable lessons through adversity and afflictions. Still, sometimes, we will not receive the experience because we are too busy fighting against the form of instruction that God has judged fit for us to mature and prepare us for glory. Suffering is not the only way we learn, and I believe that it's not even God's first choice as a lesson plan, but because we are so stubborn at times, we must go through pain to get to glory.

> *11 Now, discipline always seems painful rather than pleasant at the time, but later, it yields the peaceful fruit of righteousness to those trained by it.*
> **(Hebrews 12:11)**

The discipline of God is meant to afflict our flesh so that our spirit may mature. Remember that the author of Hebrews has referred to a race in this chapter, not a physical race but a spiritual race. In a physical race, the runners must pace themselves and breathe properly so that they may be able to endure whatever obstacles the course may offer. The pacing and breathing correspond to the length of the race. If it is a 40-yard dash, the runners can just run as fast and as hard as they want. But if it is a mile or longer, the runners must pace themselves and breathe properly to finish the race. The runner paces himself by running at a steady speed rather than bolting from the starting blocks to give himself the best chance to finish the race. In a race of runners, the goal is to win the race, but it is also quite encouraging to complete a run on your feet, such as a 26-kilometer race. There is a significant amount of discipline needed to complete a long run, and afterward, the body will ache for days, but the sense of accomplishment supersedes the pain.

As Christians, we are asked to finish a race that we began when we accepted Christ as our Lord and Savior. Patience and perseverance are to the spiritual race, what pace and proper breathing are to the physical competition. Patience is how we pace ourselves through our Christian lives, and perseverance is how we breathe properly to get through our faith's spiritual taxing during the race. The goal of physical competition is to reach the finish line. Being first matters to some degree, but finishing means a lot also. The purpose of our Christian race is to achieve holiness.

We are all winners in this race if we allow the discipline of God to help us finish the race. The competition ends when we can stand before God in all of God's glory. We often complain that our suffering is too great and forget that we have a leader who ran the race before us and made available a "How to Book" on finishing the Christian race. Jesus is the leader, and the "How to Book" is the Holy Bible. Jesus Christ ran this race before us, enduring trials that would discourage even the most faithful among us. Whenever we feel like we cannot go on, we can look at Christ and know that He ran the race to holiness before us and was rewarded by being placed at the right hand of God.

Christ is our encouragement. We can finish the race and reach holiness if we follow Christ in service, suffering, and obedience. Affliction is painful to our flesh, but we must endure this pain to get to glory, and God's glory will neutralize the sting. Neutralizing the pain comes through faith. The problem does not go away, but we can overcome it when our faith helps us endure affliction and produces the fruit of righteousness. The fruit of God's righteousness is peace. Patience during God's discipline provides stability, and this is the key to getting through our training and reaching holiness so that we may stand before God.

6

The Purifying and Strengthening of Faith

I've been taught that we suffer afflictions because of sin. As I matured in my adult life, I realized that not all suffering could be traced back to specific sins or consequences of actions. Often, we see children suffering, and they could not have done anything to bring about the affliction because they were too young. In Chicago, I have known devout Christians with a gift for giving and a profound love for the Lord, who suffer hardships inexplicably while serving God. Watching people who strive for goodness and innocent children suffer helped me realize that difficulties are not always a result of our sins but are often used to purify and strengthen our faith for the glory of God.

1 Peter 1:3-7

Living Hope

The First Letter of Peter, written to the members of a Jewish community who had recently converted to Christianity, was written to explain the Doctrines of Christianity to this audience. This letter also helps these new converts have peace while enduring slander from those who were not eager to embrace Christianity. My reason for using this letter is as I believe Peter intended, and that is to prepare our Christian community for the suffering that is inevitable because of the forces of evil that rise whenever a community of Christians chooses to set themselves apart for the glory and service of our Lord and Savior Jesus Christ. Patience and perseverance are essential to our faith as Christians.

In the early days of the expansion of the church, Christians were viewed as unpatriotic because they refused to take part in the ceremonies of the emperor and state gods. Their moral character and secret meetings kept them from engaging in mainstream activities, and rumors developed. There was growing suspicion and hostility against Christians, which led to persecution. Peter writes this pastoral letter to encourage Christians of the hope that is in Christ. In this letter, Peter reminds the community of Christians that living in a pagan society calls for humility and submission.

When we focus on Christ, we are free to commit ourselves to obedience and holiness during our suffering. It is common for Christians to suffer injustice as Christ did, and like Christ, we must endure and be obedient to God. Sometimes, we suffer despite doing what is right. When this happens, we are to have no fear, for God is with us. We are to remember the example of our Lord Jesus. He suffered injustice yet persisted in His teachings of hope. When we stay hopeful during our suffering, people will wonder why we are still hopeful, and this will open doors for giving witness to the reason for our hope, and that is Christ. We must suffer from a clear conscience, giving no time to negative thoughts about our suffering. Let us focus on the purpose of our pain instead of the pain. We should rejoice when we suffer as Christians and remember that our sorrow will lead to eternal glory with God.

My focus here is on verses 6 and 7 after Peter has just described the inheritance that the audience has received through the grace and mercy of God. In these two verses, Peter acknowledges that there are afflictions within this community of Christians but encourages them that there is always a reason to rejoice amid hardship. This joy is manifested through the conduct, praise, and gratitude of the Christian. The greatest pleasure of a faithful Christian comes in the knowledge of godly rewards because of their relationship with God. The Christian who can praise God and rejoice amid adversity truly exemplifies God's passion that is required to share in the blessings of God.

In life, there are great trials and tribulations, and these increase for Christians. In the 9th Chapter of the Letter to the Romans, Paul writes, ***"[2]I have great sorrow and unceasing anguish in my heart."*** He refers to the Hebrews, who are his compatriots but have not accepted Christ as their Savior. Paul would prefer that everyone accept the Doctrine of Christianity, but that is not realistic. Although he felt sorrow, he found within himself the strength to rejoice and preach The Gospel and Precepts of Christ, an example that although we are afflicted with grief and anguish as humans, these sorrows and afflictions cannot overshadow the blessings waiting for us as Christians. Although the afflictions and trials of Christians are heavy, they pale in comparison to eternity with God. Character is built through adversity, so it will serve us well to realize that gain will always surpass the pain, no matter how difficult the trial may be.

Faith is the most significant attribute of a serious Christian. Trials test our faith and are necessary to solidify our faith. We must be battle-tested to know who we are in Christ. While growing up in Chicago, I went to nine grammar schools, and I had to fight because I was always the new kid in school. When I transferred from the first school that I attended (Lowell), located on Hirsch and Spaulding, and I enrolled at (Avondale) on Sawyer and George, I was nervous because I was going to meet new kids, and I didn't know if they would like me or want to fight me. I prepared myself for every scenario that may present itself. I had a plan for everything until I got into a fight on my first day of school.

As a Christian, you may have a plan for your salvation. But will that plan hold up when you get stuck in the chest? I learned that lesson at eight years old. Today I am 59 years old, and I have had Multiple Sclerosis for 30 years. My plans have changed regarding a career, a spouse, and children, but my faith has increased, and I am closer to God than I would have been without the trials and afflictions.

Let us picture the day when we rise to be with God. How will we face our Pure and Holy God if we are not purified by trials here on earth? As gold is purified by fire so we must also be purified by fire before we ascend to the place that God has prepared for us.

A Man Born Blind Receives Sight

> *1 As he walked along, he saw a man blind from birth. 2 His disciples asked him, "Rabbi, who sinned, this man or his parents, that he was born blind?" 3 Jesus answered, "Neither this man nor his parents sinned; he was born blind so that God's works might be revealed in him.*
> **(John 9:1-3)**

This Chapter of the Gospel of John begins with a miracle that leads to conversations that try to get to the root of human suffering. It was thought that if a person was suffering physically, the affliction was due to the afflicted person's sinful acts or their parents. This way of thinking most certainly brought on thoughts of guilt and stigmatized those who suffered and their families.

As humans, we are always trying to assign meaning to things that we experience in the world. We are still blaming each other for the troubles in the world. We are physical beings, and we believe that if we suffer physical ailments, it must have a physical cause and, therefore, a medical solution. When we read the first three Gospels, we can see that the focus is on physical matters with references to the spiritual world. In the Gospel of John, the focus is on spiritual issues that help us understand the physical world.

"Rabbi, who sinned, this man or his parents, that he was born blind?" It makes us feel less vulnerable if we can understand the cause of (and thus avoid) misfortune. The fact that disaster might strike randomly is terrifying, so naturally, the Disciples of Christ inquired about the cause of the man's blindness. The question assumes that sin causes suffering. It could be the parents' sin.

Exod. 20:5 says,

> *"[5] You shall not bow down to them or worship them; for I the LORD your God am a jealous God, punishing children for the iniquity of parents, to the third and the fourth generation of those who reject me."*

A thought that's repeated in (***Exod. 34:7, Num. 14:18, and Deut. 5:9)***. Or it might be the blind man's sin. If so, his sin had to take place in the womb because he was blind from birth. Observations of the battle between Jacob and Esau in Rebecca's womb teach us that our fleshly desires are developed and acted on while still in the womb.

The blind man and his parents were accustomed to hearing that blindness is the result of sin. They assumed that the man's blindness was somehow their fault. They might have had their theory about immorality or sins that caused blindness. Each time they heard someone talk about the connection between sin and suffering, they suffered a little more. Jesus did not deny that sin causes pain. Instead, the blind man's situation gave an opportunity for Jesus to heal him, thereby revealing God's power. It is also useful to remember that our faith in adversity can be a compelling witness. However, we should not forget that there is a connection between sin and suffering. That was not true in the case of this blind man, but it is true. All sin causes pain. Jesus shows us that sin and suffering are not always related. We do the truth a disservice when we use this text to teach people that sin and suffering are not related. When I sin, I hurt those closest to me and myself as well. Children pay the price for the sins of their parents. Babies born addicted to drugs used by the mother are obvious, but the principle is true in less extreme circumstances. Jesus said that sin was not the cause of this blind man's infirmity. We must be careful about judging others. It is all too tempting to make negative judgments when we do not have all the facts.

John's Gospel followed the first three Gospels, helping the Early Church understand the persecutions that affected all followers of Christ's precepts. Let us try to imagine what it was like to be a Christian in those days. Those who opposed Christ thought they had stopped the "Anointed One" only to realize that the Anointed One's death gave birth to many anointed ones. They felt that by killing the leader of the movement, they would kill the movement. John helps us realize that the Christian Movement is a Spiritual Movement. The blind man received more than physical sight; he got a spiritual insight into the glory that awaits us as anointed ones. The glory of God revealed that Jesus did not blame man's blindness on sin but used it to help explain the existence of the spiritual world governed by the ultimate Spiritual Being.

As I mentioned above, I am 59, and I have had Multiple Sclerosis for over 30 years. It is tough living with a disability, and

I often remember playing baseball or walking down the street. I often think of what life would have been like if I had been born disabled. Those thoughts are scary. I can never really appreciate what life would have been like for me in that situation. The blind man in the Gospel of John had never seen his parents. He had never seen the sun rise or set, nor had he ever seen what he was eating. One can only try to imagine how this blind man ached to get just a glimpse of what he so often heard others speak about.

Although Christ was followed and watched by those who persecuted Him, He was compelled by love and compassion to stop and bring this poor soul out of the darkness and into the light. Twenty Centuries later, this act of love and kindness is still bringing people out of spiritual darkness and into the light of God. Christ had a lot going on in His life. He preached, taught, traveled, answered skeptics, and escaped persecutions, among other things, while never losing sight of the reason for His Incarnation and The One who sent Him. Christ shed His Blood for the cleansing of our sins, and if that were all that He did, it would have been enough, but He had another mission. That mission was to do God's business here on earth. Before we can reach the glory of resurrection, we must prepare for it. Afflictions can either prepare us for glory or push us away from it, so Christ had work to do before He gave His life to cleanse us of our sins. He had to live as an example of God's glory by doing good works here on earth so that humanity can see that not only does God want us to inherit eternal victory, but God wants us to have success in the world as well. Christ came to earth to help us understand the afflictions of the world and how these afflictions can prepare us for glory and show us how to alleviate the world's suffering in the name of God.

Why are we Christians? Is it only so that we escape eternal separation from God? That is partly correct, but what good would it be to the world if we only concern ourselves with going to Heaven and leaving the world in the same or worse condition than it was before we were called to be Christians? We can find the answer to that by following the doctrine and teachings of Christ.

Let us examine the words, Christ and Christians. The name Christ comes from the Greek word Cristos, which means "Anointed One." The word Christians means those who follow Christ's examples; therefore, the term Christians refers to "Little Anointed Ones." Christ is the main "Anointed One" who sets the standard for those of us who follow Him. The healing of the man who was born blind serves as an example that no matter how busy we are in the world preaching, teaching, and escaping the persecutions of the world, we should never cease doing what God has called us to do. If Christ found time in His busy schedule to do the works of God, so we also must stop and do the will of the One who called us to be Christians or "Little Anointed Ones." Christ was fleeing the persecution of the Pharisees when He stopped and healed this man who was born blind. The blind man did not reach out to Christ, but Christ reached out to him.

In my situation, I have been praying to God to relieve me of my affliction (Multiple Sclerosis). Many spiritual healers, prophets, pastors, and miracle workers have prayed for me at healing services, yet I am getting worse. I thought that I did not have enough faith. I was not wise in the ways of God at that time, so I believed that I did not have enough faith. Now, I understand that God has called me to dispel those erroneous teachings. I will suffer this and other afflictions until I am prepared to stand before God, purified of all earthly desires and contaminants.

7

Our Trials Contribute to Our Good

In the Church at Rome, there were tensions between the Christian converts, who were Jews, and Gentiles, who came together to worship Christ. Paul writes a letter to help them understand that they are a congregation noted for their faith (Romans 1:8) and that Christians, whether Jew or Gentile, require the righteousness that God gives. But this righteousness must be reflected in the life of a Christian.

One of the tensions between the converts in the Church in Rome was the Law of the Jewish Text (Old Testament) and the Faith of The Books written after the Crucifixion of Jesus, The New Testament. The Jewish converts argued that the Law should be of primary concern, and the Gentiles argued that faith was of significant interest. Paul reconciles the Old Testament Law and the New Testament Faith by explaining that in Judaism, the Righteousness of God required following the Laws of God. After the Crucifixion of Christ, righteousness required knowing the Law and being like God in our motives and actions in our relationships with each other.

> *"Therefore, since we are justified by faith, we have peace with God through our Lord Jesus Christ, [2] through whom we have obtained access to this grace in which we stand; we boast in our hope of sharing the glory of God. [3] And not only that, but we also boast in our sufferings, knowing that suffering produces endurance, [4] and endurance produces character, and character produces hope, [5] and hope does not disappoint us, because God's love has been poured into our hearts through the Holy Spirit that has been given to us."*
> **(Romans 5:1-5)**

"Therefore" (v.1) points back to the foundation that Paul established in chapters 1- 4 that none are righteous (3:9-20), but God justifies Christians as a gift (3:24), a reality that Christians show by faith (4:13-25). God's acceptance of us is not partial but total. As Paul made clear in verses 3:21-26, our faith gives us access to that grace (3:26)

"We have peace with God through our Lord Jesus Christ" (v.1). In the context of this verse, "peace with God" means being in harmony with God in spirit. Not only should we follow the written law but also the spirit of the law. That means to have God's laws written in your heart so that you can live God's laws and be led by God's Spirit. While a harmonious relationship with God naturally leads to inner peace, it is peace with God that Paul is describing here. We can have peace with God only because of the work of ***"our Lord Jesus Christ."***

"Through whom we have obtained access to this grace in which we stand" (v.2).

Through sacrifice, Christ ushers us into the presence of ***"this grace in which we stand."*** Grace is not just something for which we hope but is something that we already have. The Grace that we have is so great that Paul calls it ***"this grace in which we stand."***

"And we boast in our hope of sharing the glory of God" (v.2).

Paul has spoken earlier in this epistle of boasting but never favorably. Paul's earlier references had to do with our boasting of our works ***(2:17-23; 3:27; 4:2),*** and we have done nothing that justifies boasting. However, it is proper for us to boast of what God has done for us. Such boasting is a kind of proclamation that spreads the Word of God. ***We boast in our sufferings" (v.3).*** Why would someone boast about pain? God promises that there are blessings after suffering. We have a greater appreciation for the Sun after a storm. Likewise, we as Christians should have a greater appreciation for the Son (i.e., the Son of God) during and after our suffering.

In his Second Letter to Timothy, Paul speaks of suffering for Christ. ***"I know the one in whom I have put my trust, and I am***

sure that he can guard until that day what I have entrusted to him" (2 Timothy 1:12). In Romans 5:3-5, Paul outlines the Blessings that come through suffering. ***"Suffering produces endurance, and endurance produces character, and character produces hope, and hope does not disappoint us."*** Paul is saying that endurance produces a tested or a proven character, and after that, the character overcomes suffering with hope**. *"And hope does not disappoint us because God's love has been poured into our hearts through the Holy Spirit that has been given to us" (v.5)*.** No matter what happens, God loves us. We are beloved sons and daughters whom God will never abandon. God supports the birds of the air and the lilies of the field so we can be sure that God will provide for us ***(Matthew 6:25-34)***.

All roads can lead to God if we submit to God and allow God to work things out. Our experiences can either bring us closer to God or push us further from God. God empathizes with us in our suffering and allows our pain to work for our benefit. According to Paul, when we are in trials, and we pray, [26] ***Likewise the Spirit helps us in our weakness; for we do not know how to pray as we ought, but that very Spirit intercedes with sighs too deep for words.*** [27] ***And God, who searches the heart, knows what is the mind of the Spirit because the Spirit intercedes for the saints according to the will of God (Romans 8:26-27).*** It is our relationship with God that allows us to be victorious amid our sorrow.

Future Glory

> *"[18] I consider that the sufferings of this present time are not worth comparing with the glory that God will reveal to us."* **(ROMANS 8:18-27)**

Paul compares our present suffering with our future glory and determines that joy in heaven far outweighs our pain. Knowing this helps us put the difficulties of life in perspective and keeps us from despair. Of course, not all problems are equal. One person might suffer by no fault of their own. Another person might suffer because of their behavior. No matter the reason for the suffering, if it leads to a life of communication with God through Prayer, Worship, and Bible Study, it can lead to Eternity with God. In other words, all suffering has the potential to move us in the direction of glory.

> *"[19] For the creation waits with eager longing for the revealing of the children of God; [20] for the creation was subjected to futility, not of its own will but by choice of the one who submitted it, in hope [21] that the creation itself will be set free from its bondage to decay and will obtain the freedom of the glory of the children of God. Now, know that the whole creation has been groaning in labor pains until now; [23] and not only the creation but we, who have the first fruits of the Spirit, groan inwardly while we wait for*

> *adoption, the redemption of our bodies. [24] For in hope we were saved. Now, hope that is seen is not hope. For who hopes for what is seen? [25] But if we hope for what we do not see, we wait for it with patience."*
>
> *"[26] Likewise, the Spirit helps us in our weakness; for we do not know how to pray as we ought, but that very Spirit intercedes with sighs too deep for words. [27] And God, who searches the heart, knows what is the mind of the Spirit because the Spirit intercedes for the saints according to the will of God."*

"Likewise, the Spirit helps us in our weakness" (v.26). The word ***"Likewise"*** links this verse to those that precede it. In v.18, Paul spoke of ***"the sufferings of this present time"*** and went on to talk about creation waiting ***"with eager longing" (v.19)*** to ***"be set free from its bondage to decay" (v.21)***. Paul said that all creation groans in pain ***(v.22)***, as do ***we "who have the first fruits of the Spirit, groan inwardly while we wait for adoption, the redemption of our bodies" (v.23)***. Paul spoke of our ***"hope for what we do not see,"*** telling us that ***"we wait for it with patience"(v.25)***. It is during this suffering, groaning, and waiting that the Spirit intercedes for us (v.26) ***"for we do not know how to pray as we ought, but that very Spirit intercedes with sighs too deep for words" (v.26)***.

Sometimes, when we pray, we know exactly what we want to say and what we want God to do. Other times, we find ourselves so overwhelmed that we can only pray, "God, help me" or "God, forgive me." The good news is that, just as God has the grace to provide access to Salvation, he can hear prayers when we do not know what to say. ***"And God, who searches the heart, knows what the mind of the Spirit is because the Spirit intercedes for the saints according to the will of God" (v.27).***

> *"[28] We know that all things work together for good for those who love God, who are called according to his purpose. [29] For those whom he foreknew, he also predestined to conform to the image of his Son in order that he might be the firstborn within a large family. [30] And those whom he predestined he also called; and those whom he called he also justified, and those whom he justified he also glorified."*
> **(ROMANS 8:28-30)**

If the Spirit intercedes for us in prayer, then why is it that so many Christians suffer afflictions and trials? Just because we continue in our suffering does not mean that the intercession of the Spirit is in vain. Spirit's intervention ensures that all will be well, and whatever our afflictions, it will work out for our benefit if the Spirit intercedes for us. ***"For those who love God, who are called according to his purpose" (v.28).*** This promise does not apply to everyone. Only the person who loves God and is called according to God's purpose is assured that God will transform his/her lousy situation to bring about a good result. God searches our hearts during our suffering, and the Spirit intercedes for those who are genuinely humbled and ready for a change.

A genuinely contrite heart belongs to sanctified Christians who love God to the point of turning everything over to God entirely and acknowledging God's Sovereignty (i.e., Supreme Excellence). That makes us called according to God's purpose. We make the best out of any situation. If our situation brings us to God with a contrite heart, then whatever the case, it has worked for our benefit. Afflictions, trials, tribulations, and discipline work to separate us from sin and bring us closer to God, therefore preparing us for glory if we genuinely love God in our hearts.

The Jewish People believe that they are predestined to be God's People, and Paul was familiar with this as Paul was Jewish. However, Paul set out to include the Gentiles as God's People through Christ. God has a divine purpose for us, and that is our justification and glorification. We are to conform to Christ so that we may become part of God's Kingdom. According to the Book of Genesis, God created us in His image, but Adam distorted and broke that image in the Garden of Eden. God will restore us to His image if we become like Christ. God wants us to bear the image of Christ to prepare for glory.

8

We Always Have a Way Out

Paul set up a church in the City of Corinth ***(Acts 18)***. We currently have two letters written to the church in Corinth by Paul, and they are 1st Corinthians and 2nd Corinthians. In 1st Corinthians, Paul addresses disputes and problems within the congregation. In this letter, Paul deals with one flaw after another. Problems give this letter its structure. This letter reminds us that living together as Christians has always been a challenge. Our commitment to Christ does not exempt us from difficulties and struggles.

No church is perfect, but Christians should live in spiritual growth and harmony because God always offers us a resolution to our challenges, struggles, and difficulties. The problem-solving principles in 1st Corinthians can apply to any congregation at any time. The problems in the church of Corinth were unity, sin, divorce, doctrine, women in worship, spirituality, and the importance of the Resurrection in Christianity. This letter serves as an example that God always supplies a way out, no matter what the struggle.

Whenever we go through troubles or temptations, we are to look for the way out because God will not let us suffer or be tempted beyond what we can manage. God always provides us with an opportunity to rely on faith to get us through our struggles and temptations, but we must believe that God can deliver us if we live by faith. As human beings, we are all vulnerable to temptation, so we should be careful not to expose ourselves to temptation. Temptations and struggles will find us, but God is faithful and provides us with the way out.

> "[13] *No testing has overtaken you that is not common to everyone. God is faithful, and he will not let you be tested beyond your strength, but with the testing, he will also provide the way out so that you may be able* to *endure it.*"
> **(1st Corinthians 10:13)**

When we are in trouble, we feel hopeless. God does not want us to feel lost, so God will not allow our problems to overcome our strengths, or God will give us more power to deal with our problems. We will never be without hope in any situation so long as we are in Christ. Since human beings are vulnerable to temptations and difficulties, we need to be committed to Christ so that when temptations and adversities strike, we can rely on God to weaken the situation or strengthen us. This verse gives comfort to all who are in Christ who struggle with trials or temptation. It is also an excellent verse to minister to those without Christ in a world without hope.

If we put our strength and faith in human beings or in the solutions that the world offers us, we will surely perish under our troubles and temptations. However, this verse states that God is faithful, so it would be fair to say that if we make a total commitment to Christ, God will empower us to endure and overcome all things that can cause us spiritual harm. God knows what we will have to face in this world and has prepared us a way out, a way to overcome and use adversity for our benefit.

Relying on God while in Great Stress

In 2nd Corinthians 1:8-11, Paul writes that even he has been depressed and stressed. When I am attacked, my immediate response is to bring my strengths and accomplishments to the forefront to show that I am strong. In 2nd Corinthians, Paul teaches me that regardless of my achievements and perceived strengths, real power is revealed when I acknowledge that I am strongest when I accept my weaknesses and submit to God. We are too quick to try to overcome despair and desperation on our own and too slow to offer up our weaknesses to God. I am Puerto Rican, and in our culture, a man should never show weakness, and a woman should rely on a man to protect her. In 2nd Corinthians, Paul teaches by example when he openly shares his weaknesses with us. Paul is a strong, confident, well-educated, articulate, and faithful man of God who set up churches throughout Asia and went to prison for the sake of preaching the Gospel of Christ. Yet, he was not ashamed to recognize when he was stressed and pressured. Paul encourages us to offer up all our weaknesses and strengths to God, and God will help us change the world.

> "[8] *We do not want you to be unaware, brothers and sisters, of the affliction we experienced in Asia, for we were so utterly, unbearably crushed that we despaired of life itself.*
> [9] *Indeed, we felt that we had received the death sentence to rely not on ourselves but on God, who raises the dead.* [10]
> *He who rescued us from so deadly a peril will continue to save us; on him, we have set our hope that he will save us again,* [11] *as you also join in helping us by your prayers, so that many will give thanks on our behalf for the blessing granted us through the prayers of many."*
> **(2nd Corinthians 1:8-11)**

As ministers, we hope that others benefit from our suffering. Paul hopes that by freely writing about his pain, the members of the Church in Corinth will be able to endure anything that may come against them by just remembering that even those who are always attending to God's affairs have suffered and will continue to suffer. Still, they can overcome it by offering up all their suffering to God.

It is so hard to let go and let God deal with our troubles, which is why we are in constant struggle. Could it be that our reluctance to rely on God is the cause of our perpetual shortcomings? As humans, we are in continual need of deliverance, and Paul is teaching us to let God be in total control of our lives, and we will need nothing. Our lives will never be perfect, but our God always has been and always will be.

Strength in Weakness

Real Strength

> *"12 1 It is necessary to boast; nothing is to be gained by it,*
> *but I will go on to visions and revelations of the Lord. 2 I*
> *know a person in Christ who fourteen years ago was*
> *caught up to the third heaven—whether in the body or out*
> *of the body I do not know; God knows. 3 And I know that*
> *such a person—whether in the body or out of the body I do*
> *not know; God knows— 4 was caught up into Paradise and*
> *heard things that are not to be told, that no mortal is*
> *permitted to repeat. 5 On behalf of such a one, I will boast,*
> *but I will not boast on my behalf, except my weaknesses. 6*
> *but if I wish to boast, I will not be a fool, for I will be*
> *speaking the truth. But I refrain from it so that no one may*
> *think better of me than what is seen in me or heard from*
> *me, 7 even considering the exceptional character of the*
> *revelations. Therefore, to keep me from being too elated, a*
> *thorn was given me in the flesh, a messenger of Satan to*
> *torment me, to keep me from being too elated. 8 Three times*
> *I appealed to the Lord about this, that it would leave me, 9*
> *but he said to me, "My grace is sufficient for you, for power*
> *is made perfect in weakness." So, I will boast all the more*
> *gladly of my weaknesses, so that the power of Christ may*

dwell in me. [10] Therefore, I am content with weaknesses, insults, hardships, persecutions, and calamities for the sake of Christ; for whenever I am weak, then I am strong." **(2nd Corinthians 12:1-10)**

In the 12th Chapter of 2nd Corinthians, Paul teaches us that God uses our weakest moments to make us more dependable and spiritually compelling. According to Paul, he had a thorn in his flesh to keep him from being prideful and boastful. The thorn caused great humility and made him appear to be weak. It was at his most vulnerable point that Paul realized that his weakness and humility made him stronger. God had taken weakness and made it a source of strength. Paul never reveals what the thorn was, leaving us to be able to apply the thorn in the flesh concept to whatever may touch our lives and function as a hindrance in our service to God. This concept applies to anything that makes us appear weak in the eyes of those to whom we minister. Paul prayed that God might remove it, but God's reply was, ***"My grace is sufficient for you, for power is made perfect in weakness."***

Our weaknesses can be a call for us to rely on God, who shows us throughout the Bible that man looks at physical appearances, but God looks at the heart of man. We look at the present, and God looks at the future.

When our weaknesses are exposed, everyone can see that God does mighty things through us so that no one can take credit but

God. When we learn to rely on Christ and not on our abilities, we are more effective in our ministries and all our relationships in general. Paul was a Christian, yet he remained afflicted. I thought that my faith was weak, but Paul's faith was not weak. God's response to me was that faithful Christians could suffer poor health and other problems without the cause being faithlessness or sin. We can endure all things if we keep in mind that there is a purpose for our struggles and God's strength is perfect through our afflictions. Do not be afraid to suffer.

In the first seven verses of 2nd Corinthians Chapter 12, we get an example of how we should testify in the Church. I used to testify to the remarkable things that I have accomplished in my life. I once heard a brother say that he will give glory to God, but the victory is his. I guess one could argue that success is ours on earth, and the glory belongs to God, but in this part of 2nd Corinthians, Paul teaches me that success is God's as well as the glory.

I have four diplomas in the social sciences, including psychology, sociology, social work, and divinity; although I feel a great sense of accomplishment, I am quadriplegic. I have limited use of my right arm, so to God be all the glory and victories. A proper testimony would be for me to offer up my accomplishments and afflictions to God and feed God's People. I am disabled, alone, and in pain, but in Christ, I am able, spiritually prosperous, in the company of God, Christ, and the Holy Spirit, and the pain keeps me firmly grounded. To God, be all the victory and glory.

I believe that while we can achieve success on earth through our efforts, the ultimate glory belongs to God. This perspective emphasizes humility and gratitude, recognizing that our abilities and opportunities are gifts from God.

Achieving goals, overcoming challenges, and experiencing personal victories are important aspects of our lives. These successes are the result of hard work, talent, and perseverance, but the true glory belongs to God, as He is the source of all good things. This view encourages me to give thanks and praise to God for the blessings and successes that I experience.

Paul prays for God to heal him, but God allows it to persist. Instead, Paul is to rely on God's Grace. I often pray for my affliction to leave me, but I remain afflicted. Why? What is the point of praying in faith if the situation stays the same? I have asked this question, and I would like to offer an answer. While praying to God for healing, I often wondered why I even bothered, and then I realized that since my diagnosis, I have spent more time praying and listening to God. If our suffering, troubles, and afflictions can bring us closer to God, then, in this case, the ends justify the means. God will prepare us for glory by any means necessary.

9

Patience Built through Trials

James, the younger brother of Jesus, was a prominent leader in the early Christian church in Jerusalem. The Church in Jerusalem was founded shortly after the Crucifixion of Christ, and there were many persecutions against the Early Christian Church at that time. Early Christians faced significant hardships, including imprisonment, torture, and martyrdom, for their faith. As the Pastor of the Church of Jerusalem, James was concerned with the faith of his congregation during the persecutions. James was teaching the group how to live as Christians in the face of increasing persecution.

The book of James in the New Testament is rich with practical teachings and doctrines that guide Christian living. Here are seven of the key doctrines and themes:

1. Faith and Works: James emphasizes that genuine faith is action. He argues that faith without works is dead (James 2:14-26).

2. Wisdom from Above: The book highlights the importance of seeking wisdom from God, which is pure, peaceable, gentle, and full of mercy (James 1:5; 3:13-18).
3. Perseverance through Trials: James teaches that trials and testing of faith produce perseverance, leading to spiritual maturity (James 1:2-4).
4. Wealth and Oppression: The book addresses the issues of wealth and poverty, warning against favoritism towards the rich and encouraging care for the poor (James 2:1-7; 5:1-6).
5. Control of the Tongue: James stresses the importance of controlling our speech, as the tongue can cause great harm if not restrained (James 3:1-12).
6. Prayer and Healing: The book underscores the power of prayer, especially in the context of healing and forgiveness (James 5:13-16).
7. Humility and Submission to God: James calls for humility and submission to God, resisting the devil and drawing near to God (James 4:7-10).

These doctrines offer practical guidance for living out one's faith in everyday life.

James believes in faith that works. True Christian Faith is a faith that transforms us and our way of life. Worship in the life of a believer is shown by producing the fruits of a person committed to Christ.

Faith and Wisdom

"[2]My brothers and sisters, whenever you face trials of any kind, consider it nothing but joy, [3] because you know that the testing of your faith produces endurance; [4] and let endurance have its full effect, so that you may be mature and complete, lacking in nothing. "
(James 1:2-4)

Why me? I have asked that question in the face of trials and afflictions. We expect terrible things to happen to those who do not have a relationship with God. We even tell people that pain is a result of separation from God. People look toward God to alleviate their pain, only to become disillusioned when the suffering does not cease but increases. Many who seek God to be relieved of suffering give up on God when the problem continues. So, what is the point? Why seek God if we will suffer just the same as those who do not seek God?

The Book of James teaches that not only will trials continue while we are in God's will, but the tests may increase for Christians. The best Christians will have to endure hardships. The "Why me?" question is answered in the Book of James with "Why not you?" and "Especially you!" Who can deal with trials better than those who have faith in and serve the Creator of all things? Trials and afflictions do not cease when we come to God, but hopelessness does cease to be part of our lives when we submit to

God's will, for it is in God's will that we find God's Love, Grace, Mercy, and Strength. Imagine suffering with no hope in sight. That is the difference between suffering in God's will and suffering outside of God's will. Our trials are in God's will when we suffer in Christ.

The Book of James calls us to be joyful during our suffering, and for a long time, I had a problem with that concept until I realized that my trials and afflictions caused me to speak with God more often. It was not always joyful expressions that I shared with God because, to be quite honest, I was bitterly angry with God. But the fact that I was directing my anger toward God let me know that I thought highly of God and believed that God could resolve all my suffering. We must not allow our pain to cause us to become sad, depressed, or angry because that can lead to sin.

As Christians, we view trials and suffering as expressions of God's love and not God's anger. We suffer for the sake of righteousness. I was able to feel God's presence in my life more clearly amid my suffering. Suffering can bring us closer to God. As Christians, we should welcome anything that brings us closer to God with immense joy. Trials and afflictions can be great tools for learning if we submit to God's will and acknowledge the Sovereignty of God. Trials produce patience, and patience is a virtue.

Trials are a Good Gift

James encourages the Christian Community to greet trials with joy and to be aware of their potential benefits. While in trials, we ask God for direction but tend to forsake obedience for doing things our way. When we ask God for guidance, we must be obedient to God so that we may receive God's Guidance.

Trial and Temptation

"12 Blessed is anyone who endures temptation. Such a one has stood the test and will receive the crown of life that the Lord has promised to those who love him. 13 No one, when tempted, should say, "God is tempting me;" for God cannot be tempted by evil, and he himself tempts no one. 14 But one is tempted by one's desire, being lured and enticed by it; 15 then, when that desire has conceived, it gives birth to sin, and that sin, when it is fully grown, gives birth to death. 16 Do not be deceived, my beloved. 17 Every generous act of giving, with every perfect gift, is from above, coming down from the father of lights, with whom there is no variation or shadow due to change. 18 In fulfillment of his purpose, he gave birth by the word of truth so that we would become the kind of first fruits of his creatures.
(James 1:12-18)

Let us now learn the difference between trials and temptations. Trials are external, while temptations are internal. As humans, we believe that God tests us and tempts us, and I want to clarify what James teaches us. God will not tempt us to do evil. Doing what is not in God's will is to work against God. Falling into temptation is a result of not following God's guidance and doing our own thing. Trials can result from falling into temptation, but God had nothing to do with the temptation. God will allow the persecution, so we may turn from our wicked ways and receive the excellent gift that trials can lead to if we endure and stay faithful to God.

Suffering and persecution can lead to eternal blessings. God allows trials, but temptations come from our flesh and sinful desires. We must commit to God and righteous living, and this is by practicing God's Word. By practicing God's Word, we become doers of God's Word instead of just hearing God's Word. Many have read or listened to the Word of God, but few are those who practice God's Word (i.e., The Bible).

10

Be Serious and Repent under Discipline

Rebuke and discipline come to those who are loved by God. God spiritually enriches our lives. For our lives to be spiritually enriched, we must obey God's Statutes. When we are disobedient, we are rebuked and disciplined for our spiritual benefit.

The Book of Revelation mentions a Church in Laodicea that was neither cold nor hot but lukewarm in its commitment to God. The Book of Revelation makes it clear that Jesus will spit a lukewarm church out of His mouth. In today's world, we have people who are straddling a fence between a genuine commitment to Christ (hot) and no commitment to Christ (cold). When I was growing up in Chicago, we called that "half-stepping" because they could not commit, yet they seemed like they might be willing to commit. Today, we take pride in our material well-being even while we are in spiritual poverty. Jesus is eager to enter our lives, but we must commit, or God will rebuke and discipline us until we commit. The message to the Church in Laodicea is in Revelation 3:14-22.

The Message to Laodicea

> *"[14] And to the angel of the church in Laodicea write: The words of the Amen, the faithful and true witness, the origin of God's creation: 15" I know your works; you are neither cold nor hot. I wish that you were either cold or hot. [16] So, because you are lukewarm and neither cold nor hot, I am about to spit you out of my mouth. [17] For you say, 'I am rich, I have prospered, and I need nothing.' You do not realize that you are wretched, pitiable, poor, blind, and naked. [18] Therefore I counsel you to buy from me gold refined by fire so that you may be rich, and white robes to clothe you and to keep the shame of your nakedness from being seen, and salve to anoint your eyes so that you may see. [19] I reprove and discipline those whom I love. Be earnest, therefore, and repent· [20] Listen! I am standing at the door, knocking; if you hear my voice and open the door, I will come to you and eat with you, and you with me."*
> **(Revelation 3:14-22)**

When we read the messages sent to these churches in Revelation, we can see that the churches are commended in some areas but rebuked in other areas except for the last two Churches, Philadelphia and Laodicea. There are no criticisms in the message to Philadelphia, and there are no commendations in the Letter to Laodicea, an example of Christ's Love. Even when there is nothing good to say about us (Laodicea), Christ is still willing to forgive us if we repent.

The Love of Christ is steady and unchangeable. The Christians of Laodicea took pride in their wealth and self-sufficiency without seeing their spiritual poverty. People can be blinded by good health and prosperity.

Being indecisive about serving Christ is equal to being indifferent to His Sacrifice on the Cross. The Sacrifice of Christ on the Cross deserves our complete attention. Christ gives us His full attention when we come to Him, seeking grace and mercy. Could you imagine if the Love of Christ for us was lukewarm? Christ did not half-step His way up The Road to Calvary. He was not indecisive. While in the Garden of Gethsemane, Jesus threw Himself on the ground and prayed that, if it were possible, the hour might pass from Him. He said, ***"Abba, Father, for you all things are possible; remove this cup from me; yet, not what I want, but what you want."*** He could have said Abba, Father, I know you love the people of this world, but I can take them or leave them. He could have backed out, but He acknowledged that while His flesh was weak, His Passion was strong when He said: ***"The spirit indeed is willing, but the flesh is weak."*** He continues to pray and resolves to be taken without a fight. This is a demonstration of the zeal of Christ's Love for us. Christ understands that the flesh is weak; therefore, He gives us the chance to commit before Judgment Day.

When I was healthy, I was living wildly. I only looked to God when I was in danger. When I prayed, I could not hear God reply to me because of all the worldly distractions. I was diagnosed with Multiple Sclerosis and told that it was a degenerative disease and that I would worsen as time passed; I cried before God in prayer and asked why? God responded, and for the first time, I heard the reply. God said that I would go to one of the world's top universities and study psychotherapy and ministry and feed His people. At the time, I had no idea what that meant, but I committed to Christ and let God lead me. I did not know how it would happen because, according to the Christians in the churches that I attended and my family members, I was an incorrigible heathen. I became sober, repented under discipline, and registered at Wilbur Wright College in Chicago. It had been 13 years since I graduated from Carl Schurz High School, and I did not know how I would attend one of the best universities in the world, but my disability was meant to correct my wild ways, so I pressed on. I graduated from Wright College with honors and moved on to DePaul University in Lincoln Park, Chicago. I graduated from DePaul with a BA in Psychology and a minor in Sociology and was awarded The Reverend Ben Richardson's Humanitarian Award in 1999. Then, I studied at the University of Chicago, and I graduated with two master's degrees, one in Clinical Social Service Administration and another in Divinity.

When we humble ourselves and repent under discipline, we make ourselves available for God's purpose. Not bad for a person with my history, but it is only the beginning of what God is doing in my life. I was serious and repented under discipline. The beauty of it all is that God has no favorites. I made God my favorite. If you get serious about the present state of your commitment to Christ, God will work miracles in your life. Get hot for God!

We have a wonderful counselor in Christ. He continues to counsel us even though we are lost in our vanity and thoughts of self-reliance. We must rely on Christ to gain true riches. Christ offers us real wealth if we separate ourselves from sin and worldly wealth. Remember that the Church at Laodicea was wealthy financially but poor spiritually. Christ recommended that they buy His gold to become rich. The gold that Christ is offering is not of this world and cannot be purchased with the currency of this world. The gold that Christ offers is spiritual gold tried by fire. He gives riches consisting of victory in our lives against all evil and Eternity in God's Presence. These riches are more significant than any riches that can be obtained in this world. But the wealth of Christ comes at a price. We must depart from sin and egotistical ways.

Arrogance and narcissism must be given up to Christ before achieving victory on earth and Eternity with God.

> *"[19] I reprove and discipline those whom I love. Be earnest, therefore, and repent."* **(Revelation 3:19)**

At first, I thought that Christ was too harsh on the Church of Laodicea until I read further and realized that Christ had a loving message for them and us. Christ disciplines those whom He loves. If He did not love the Church of Laodicea, He would not have bothered to send them a message. If Christ did not love us, we would never have to be disciplined. When a child is undisciplined, he grows up to be unruly and ignorant. Christ would not have us be ignorant. We reflect Christ as children reflect their parents. God is the one who chastises and rebukes us for our good. When I was a child, my mother would discipline me and tell me that I would thank her later. I remember thinking, "Yeah, right." Well, I do thank her for her strict discipline because, together with God's training, I am a better man than I would have been.

> *"[21] To the one who conquers, I will give a place with me on my throne, just as I myself conquered and sat down with my father on his throne. [22] Let anyone who has an ear listen to what the Spirit is saying to the churches."*
> **(Revelation 3:21-22)**

The message closes with an eschatological promise of reward to these churches. In this message, the victory comes after the

Christians repent under discipline. The ultimate prize is to sit with Christ on the Throne of Judgment at the end of time. The message to the Church of Laodicea is meant for all Christians, especially the Christians living in the 21st Century. We are living in a time of great prosperity and technological advancement. It is easy to get distracted these days and lose sight of who we are in Christ.

Conclusion

How Does God Commune with Us When We Suffer?

Afflictions, trials, tribulations, and discipline have always been a part of life for human beings. As human beings, we can reason, and we need to assign meaning to our experiences in life. My hope in writing this book is to help the reader understand that it is more important to know that all our afflictions, trials, tribulations, and discipline can make us stronger people and prepare us to inhabit Heaven with God, Jesus, and the Holy Ghost. Our troubles can be overwhelming and disheartening if we do not believe that God takes an active role in our suffering.

Sometimes, it is hard to see how God relates to us in our afflictions, trials, tribulations, and suffering. All the pain that we experience can distract us if we stay focused on it. Still, when we see God as triune (i.e., 3 in 1), we can break down the different responsibilities of each of the three personalities of God and see how God relates to us and our suffering. God has a plan to save the world from pain. God set a plan of Salvation in motion so that none of us would perish. Jesus was the executor of the plan by His Incarnation and giving His Life so that we would be able to receive Salvation and have a relationship with God. The Holy Spirit is the enforcer of the plan by leading us to Jesus, who is the Way to God. God is one true essence and three separate persons, with Christ being the center of the Trinity. God relates to the world through the Trinity to help us get through our suffering.

Human suffering is where we can see God at work. God relates to the world by having a one-on-one relationship with every person in any situation through a Christ-centered trinity. God is present both in joy and suffering. This is accomplished through the triune nature of God. We may still suffer, but amid our pain, we must realize that Christ can connect us to God, who can help us look past the suffering and not at it. The suffering will come as Jesus said in Scripture, but we have hope in God. We can endure the pain of grief if we know that someday it will subside. This is the hope that we have in Christ. The Trinity is of utmost importance in understanding how God relates to the world and suffering.

All that we need to know about God and suffering is in Christ. Jesus is God in action. God is related to the world through Christ. If we study the Precepts of Christ, we will know what God wants for us and how God relates to us during our suffering. God has prepared a place for us in Heaven, and our experiences in life can prepare us for Heaven if we look toward the three persons who love us the most: God, Jesus, and the Holy Ghost.

Bible Verses

Here are some Bible verses from the New Revised Standard Version (NRSV) that address afflictions, trials, tribulations, and discipline:

Afflictions

"Many are the afflictions of the righteous, but the Lord rescues them from them all."
(Psalm 34:19)

"For this slight momentary affliction is preparing us for an eternal weight of glory beyond all measure."
(2 Corinthians 4:17)

"It is good for me that I was humbled, so that I might learn your statutes."
(Psalm 119:71)

Trials

"My brothers and sisters, whenever you face trials of any kind, consider it nothing but joy because you know that the testing of your faith produces endurance; and let endurance have its full effect, so that you may be mature and complete, lacking in nothing."
(James 1:2-4)

"In this, you rejoice, even if now for a little while you have had to suffer various trials, so that the genuineness of your faith—being more precious than gold that, though perishable, is tested by fire—may be found to result in praise and glory and honor when Jesus Christ is revealed."
(1 Peter 1:6-7)

Tribulations

"I have said this to you, so that in me you may have peace. In the world, you face persecution. But take courage; I have conquered the world!"
(John 16:33)

"Rejoice in hope, be patient in suffering, persevere in prayer."
(Romans 12:12)

Discipline

"My child, do not despise the Lord's discipline or be weary of his reproof, for the Lord reproves the one he loves, as a father the son in whom he delights."
(Proverbs 3:11-12)

"Now, discipline always seems painful rather than pleasant at the time, but later it yields the peaceful fruit of righteousness to those who have been trained by it."
(Hebrews 12:11)

These verses offer comfort and guidance on how to navigate through difficult times and understand the purpose behind them.

www.ingramcontent.com/pod-product-compliance
Lightning Source LLC
LaVergne TN
LVHW020644100826
845148LV00012B/2330

* 9 7 9 8 2 1 8 6 6 4 1 9 0 *